Believe in Me

Believe in Me

Sermons on the Apostles' Creed

James A. Harnish

Abingdon Press
Nashville

BELIEVE IN ME: SERMONS ON THE APOSTLES' CREED

Copyright © 1991 by Abingdon Press

This book is printed on acid-free paper.

Scripture quotations, unless otherwise indicated, are from the New Revised Standard Version Bible, copyright © 1989, by the Division of Christian Education of the National Council of the Churches of Christ in the United States of America.

Those noted GNB are from the *Good News Bible*—Old Testament: Copyright © American Bible Society 1976; New Testament: Copyright © American Bible Society 1966, 1971, 1976. Used by permission.

Those noted TLB are from *The Living Bible*, copyright © 1971 by Tyndale House Publishers, Wheaton, IL. Used by permission.

The excerpt from *For Heaven's Sake* by Helen L. Kromer, on p. 48, is copyright 1961 by Helen L. Kromer. Copyright 1963 (new material added) by Walter H. Baker Company. Reprinted by permission of Baker's Plays.

Library of Congress Cataloging-in-Publication Data

Harnish, James A.
    Believe in me: sermons on the Apostles' Creed / James A. Harnish.
       p.   cm. — (The Protestant pulpit exchange)
    Includes bibliographical references.
    ISBN 0-687-02819-1 (alk. paper)
    1. Apostles'Creed—Sermons. 2. Sermons, American, I. Title. II. Series.
BT993.2.H38 1991
238'.11—dc20   90-27663
                                                   CIP

MANUFACTURED IN THE UNITED STATES OF AMERICA

With gratitude for
Dr. Charles Killian.
You taught us to preach, to laugh, to live.
Carpe Diem

Contents

Introduction

The Foolishness of Preaching

*I*t was Saturday night. I had just put the finishing touches on a sermon with which I had been wrestling all week long. Feeling genuinely satisfied with the results and anticipating the morning ahead, I ambled out to the family room to watch a favorite television show. As I settled into an overstuffed easy chair, my elementary school teacher wife casually remarked, "I hope you realize that very few people are auditory learners."

She did not intend to burst my balloon; she was simply stating an obvious fact that any educator knows. Only a small portion of the population learns best by hearing. The vast majority are visual, or kinesthetic, learners. The case can be made that with the increasing saturation of television, the percentages are continuing to shift toward visual learning with every succeeding generation.

That was not what I needed to hear! She had pinpointed the sometimes exhausting, sometimes exhilarating irony of preaching: How do we communicate through human words the living Word of God? How do we preach to a world of visual learners? It may be a contemporary expression of what Paul called the "foolishness of our preaching" (I Cor. 1:18-25).

Add to the foolishness of how we preach the question of what we preach. A feature article on aging in a national news magazine contained this disturbing sentence: "Hardly anyone outside of divinity school is interested in eternal life." The writer assumed that theology has become the esoteric interest of a few reclusive professors who are puttering around in musty libraries, tucked away in some back corner of the university. The unquestioned assumption was that no ordinary person is really interested in theology.

There is evidence to support that assumption. Pollster George Gallup, Jr., recently told the Evangelical Press Association that the majority of Americans claim to believe in God and Jesus, but do not know the doctrines and history of their chosen "faith." Where does that leave a person who is called to preach? Are we expected to communicate theology, about which no one really cares, to people who are no longer equipped to hear?

This is a book of sermons, that strange form of verbal communication that occurs in the context of Christian worship, growing out of the life of a local congregation. Sermons ought to be heard, not read. This is auditory communication reduced to printed form. I hope that you will attempt to "hear" these sermons rather than "read" them. Their purpose is theological, attempting to help laypersons wrestle with the central affirmations of the Christian faith.

I have preached these sermons in worship at St. Luke's United Methodist Church at Windermere, a twelve-year-old congregation serving the exploding southwest corner of Orange County, Florida. At least one third of our people were not active in any church prior to coming here. Many grew up in the church as children, but left that experience behind with their high school diplomas. Some were burned by overly zealous charismatic or fundamentalist preachers. A significant number represent that growing percentage of our population that has no religious background at all. A majority are related to the tourist industry or are directly employed at the Walt Disney World or Universal Studios theme parks. They are, therefore, oriented toward visual, creative communication, all of which offers an exciting, demanding challenge to a preacher.

While preaching these sermons, I led a sermon talk-back group for "faithful skeptics" in which nothing was so sacred that it could not be questioned. The group convinced me that people *are* interested in theology. They *do* care about what they believe. They are not interested in arid discussions of abstract concepts, but they are hungry for solid theology that makes sense to them and makes a difference in their lives.

Dramatist-theologian Dorothy L. Sayers affirmed the dramatic character of Christian theology in words that are still accurate today:

> The Christian faith is the most exciting drama that ever staggered the imagination of man—and the dogma is the drama. . . . If we think it dull it is because we either have never really read those amazing documents, or have recited them so often and so mechanically as to have lost all sense of their meaning. . . . We may call that doctrine exhilarating or we may call it devastating; we may call it revelation or we may call it rubbish; but if we call it dull, then words have no meaning at all. (Dorothy L. Sayers, *Creed or Chaos* [New York: Harcourt, Brace and Company, 1949], pp. 3, 7)

Believe in Me is one preacher's offering of the product of the weekly task of preaching to pastors and laypersons who share the same struggle, with the hope that together we will experience anew the exhilarating power of the Christian faith contained in that amazing affirmation that we call the Apostles' Creed.

James A. Harnish
Orlando, Florida

"I believe . . . "

> *I know the one in whom I have put my trust,*
> *and I am sure that he is able to guard until*
> *that day what I have entrusted to him.*
> *(II Tim. 1:12)*

A Center That Will Hold

The line haunted my soul long before I knew its source: "Things fall apart; the center cannot hold." It comes from the poem "The Second Coming," written by Irish poet William Butler Yeats. This poem is considered by most critics to be great; indeed, one critic calls it "one of the great lyrics of the century . . . it rises out of difficulty and above it, and reduces the complex to a blinding simplicity" (B. L. Reid, *William Butler Yeats: The Lyric of Tragedy* [Westport, Conn.: Greenwood, 1978] p. 134).

The poem was first published in 1921, while Britain and Europe were reeling from the devastation of World War I, the Russian Revolution, and the "Easter Rebellion," which had recently rocked Ireland. Perhaps that is why the poem is pessimistic. The events of recent history had shattered the idealism of the late nineteenth century. No wonder Yeats wrote:

> The blood-dimmed tide is loosed, and everywhere
> The ceremony of innocence is drowned

No wonder he felt that "Things fall apart; the center cannot hold."

I have my own adolescent memory of that image, based on the difference between 33 RPM and 45 RPM records. One of the great mysteries of life for me is why the big records have the little holes and the little records have the big holes. My cousin had one of those nifty little 45 RPM record players with the fat spindle in the center, but we didn't have one. I remember bringing my first 45 home— it was probably Pat Boone or Ricky Nelson. I placed it on our turntable—which didn't have the fat spindle—set the needle down, and turned it on. Ricky sounded fine for the first few bars. Then the record began to slide, the needle began to wobble, and the whole thing slid all over the place.

I had never heard of William Butler Yeats, but I quickly discovered what it means to say, "Things fall apart; the center cannot hold."

What a contrast Yeats's poem is to Timothy's letter from the Apostle Paul. There are some similarities. Like Yeats, Paul was facing difficult times. He is writing from prison in Rome, and everyone has deserted him except for Luke, the faithful physician. It is a dark and dismal time. He tells Timothy: "I am already being poured out as a libation, and the time of my departure has come. I have fought the good fight, I have finished the race, I have kept the faith" (II Tim. 4:6-7). There would be good reason for this to be a depressing letter, but instead, it reverberates with this bold affirmation: "I know the one in whom I have put my trust, and I am sure that he is able to guard until that day what I have entrusted to him" (II Tim. 1:12). The Apostle had found a center that would hold, a central affirmation for his life, which filled him with confidence, even in the hour of death.

> *"If we are to find a center that will hold . . .*
> *then we must become, in the words of*
> *John Wesley, people 'of one book,' men and*
> *women whose lives are nourished by scripture."*

I pulled back from the letter and asked the questions I suspect Timothy asked: So Paul, where did you find that center? How can I develop the kind of faith that can be a solid center for my own soul? Where can I find that kind of confidence for hard and difficult times? I found Paul's answer in verses 13 and 14. First, he writes, "Hold to the standard of sound teaching that you have heard from me." In the third chapter, Paul expands on this:

> From childhood you have known the sacred writings that are able to instruct you for salvation through faith in Christ Jesus. All scripture is inspired by God and is useful for teaching, for reproof, for correction, and for training in righteousness, so that everyone who belongs to God may be proficient, equipped for every good work. (II Tim. 3:15-17)

If we are to find a center that will hold; if we are to stand up and say, "I believe . . . "; if we are to be fully equipped for the good life God intends for us, then we must become, in the words of John Wesley, people "of one book," men and women whose lives are nourished by scripture, shaped by the written witness to the living Word of God.

Let me give you a powerful illustration of this truth. In 1981 his name had not yet become a global household word; he had not yet received the Noble Peace Prize. Desmond Tutu was just a bishop in South Africa, serving as the executive secretary of the South African Council of

Churches. He was called before a Commission of Inquiry, set up to investigate the Council. Picture clearly in your mind a small black man confronting all the awesome fury of apartheid. And what did he talk about? He talked about the Bible. He said:

> You whites brought us the Bible; now we blacks are taking it seriously. We are involved with God to set us free from all that enslaves us and makes us less than what He intended us to be. . . . The Bible is the most revolutionary, the most radical book there is. If any book should be banned by those who rule unjustly and as tyrants, then it is the Bible. (Allister Sparks, *The Mind of South Africa* [New York: Alfred A. Knopf, 1990], p. 292.)

Bishop Tutu led his judges through a profound Bible study of how the God of history liberates the oppressed and concluded with this courageous affirmation, which we are now beginning to see fulfilled: "I want the Government to know now and always that I do not fear them. They are trying to defend the utterly indefensible and they will fail. They will fail because they are ranging themselves on the side of evil and injustice against the Church of God" (Sparks, *The Mind of South Africa* p. 292).

Here's the way a secular newspaper reporter described the scene: "The commissioners stared stonily ahead of them. . . . Tutu leaned back, closed the old leather-bound Bible he had been brandishing, and mopped his brow. A rearguard battle in the theological civil war had been fought and won" (Sparks, *The Mind of South Africa,* p. 292).

Any creed that dares to call itself an expression of the Christian faith must be grounded in scripture. If we are to have the kind of faith that will equip us for every kind of good deed, if we are to find a solid center that will hold us steady in difficult times, if we are to know whom we have believed, then we must read, study, discuss, devour, and nourish our souls on the witness of the written word. "Hold firmly," Paul said, "to the true words that I taught you."

> *"For Christian people, there is no belief that is not shared belief; no theology that is not born out of community; no creed that is not strengthened in friendship."*

Paul also tells Timothy to "be strong in the grace that is in Christ Jesus" (II Tim. 2:1). That sounds like friendship. You cannot read this letter without feeling the passion and intensity of Paul's friendship with Timothy. The letter over-flows with it. Paul writes: "I remember you constantly in my prayers night and day. Recalling your tears, I long to see you so that I may be filled with joy. . . . Do your best to come to me soon" (II Tim. 1:3-4; 4:9).

When was the last time you wrote a letter like that? How long has it been since you remembered the face of a friend who was so much a part of your life, so deeply bound up with your soul that you could not help thinking of him or her night and day? How long has it been since you shared someone else's tears? When was the last time you wrapped your arms around a brother or sister in the love of Christ? If you want to find a center that will hold, then practice the gift of Christian friendship.

Before someone says, "Friendship? What does that have to do with the Apostles' Creed?" let me remind you that the creed emerged out of the life of the church. The com-munity of faith came first, and the creed grew out of their life together as the declaration of their new identity as the followers of Jesus Christ in a hostile world. For Christian people, there is no belief that is not shared belief; no theology that is not born out of community; no creed that is not strengthened in friendship. As John Wesley reminded us, there is no holiness that is not social holiness.

In my years in ministry, I've seen many people face tough times. While I hate generalizations, such as "There are only two kinds of people in the world," I have become convinced as I have observed people in difficult times that there really are just two kinds of people in this world: those who discover the power of friendship and those who don't. There are those who open their lives to someone else, who allow a friend to invade the inner sanctum of their souls, who share themselves in the love of Christ. And when the tough times come, these persons find nourishment, courage, strength, and hope in their relationships. Then there are the persons who are determined to be independent, self-sufficient, to stand alone. And when difficult times come, that's exactly where they are: independent and alone.

Be strong through the grace that is ours in union with Christ Jesus. This sounds a lot like what Jesus said to his disciples on the night before he died: "Remain united to me, and I will remain united to you. . . . Remain in my love. . . . I do not call you servants any longer, because a servant does not know what his master is doing. Instead, I call you friends, because I have told you everything" (John 15:4, 9, 15 GNB).

Paul also reminds Timothy of "the help of the Holy Spirit living in us" (II Tim. 1:14). Paul thinks back to the day he laid his hands on Timothy's head and confirmed him in the faith—the way we lay our hands on the heads of youth for confirmation or on the heads of those persons whom we are setting aside for special service in the mission of the church. "I remind you to rekindle the gift of God that is within you through the laying on of my hands; for God did not give us a spirit of cowardice, but rather a spirit of power and of love and of self-discipline" (II Tim. 1:6-7).

> *"There is only one thing in this universe that is big enough to fill the empty space in our souls; it is the Spirit of God."*

I learned a long time ago that if you have a big hole in the middle of your record, you need to have a big spindle to fill it. I have since learned that there is a huge hole in the center of our souls, which can only be filled with the living, loving, life-giving Spirit of God. We try to fill it with all sorts of other things—success, power, prestige, money, sex, influence—but it is like a huge, internal sinkhole that will swallow up all the puny things we try to stuff into it, and it will leave us empty and dry.

There is only one thing in this universe that is big enough to fill the empty space in our souls; it is the Spirit of God. Pentecost has already happened. The gift has already been given. The Spirit is alive and present within and among God's people. God's Spirit is the spirit of power, love, and self-control. When we nourish the presence of the Spirit in our lives, then, regardless of whatever happens, we are never alone.

I might as well confess that there is not one original idea in this sermon. You've heard all this before. So had Timothy. That's why Paul uses the word *remember* over and over again. Most of us need to be reminded more than we need to be informed. So I want to remind you of what it takes to say, "I believe . . . " to find a center that will hold:

Hold firmly to the truth, the written witness to
   the living Word.
Remain in the love and faith that are ours in
   Christ Jesus. That's Christian friendship.
And open your life to the power of the Holy Spirit
   who lives within us.

H. G. Spafford was a businessman who lost everything in the great Chicago fire. While he was trying to rebuild his business, he sent his wife and four daughters on a voyage to Great Britain to visit relatives, planning to take a later voyage and meet them there. On November 22, 1873, there was an accident at sea: The liner was rammed by another ship and sank immediately. Mrs. Spafford was saved, but all four daughters were lost. When she arrived in England she sent a two-word telegram to her husband: "Saved alone."

Spafford took the next ship to meet her. When his ship reached the place where the ship his family traveled on had gone down, the captain notified the passengers of the location. Spafford said that he spent a sleepless night, tumbling and turning in his sorrow. Finally he wrote his feelings down, and they came out in poetry. Here is what he wrote:

When peace, like a river, attendeth my way,
When sorrows like sea billows roll;
Whatever my lot, thou hast taught me to say,
It is well, it is well with my soul.

Things do fall apart, but the center can hold!

"...in God, the Father ... Son ...Holy Spirit"

> *Go therefore and make disciples of all nations, baptizing them in the name of the Father and of the Son and of the Holy Spirit.*
> *(Matt. 28:19)*

The God Who Is There

One day a little boy came to his father and asked, "Daddy, what holds up the world?" The father, reaching back into his knowledge of mythology, said, "That's simple, my son. The world rests on the back of a very large turtle." The little boy, satisfied, walked away, but within a day or two he was back again. "But, Daddy," he asked, "what holds up the turtle?" The father, now committed to this line of reasoning, said, "My son, the turtle rests on the back of a very large tiger." Again the boy went away satisfied, at least for a few hours, until he returned to ask again, "But, Daddy, what holds up the tiger?" This time the father replied, "The tiger rests on the back of a very large elephant." As you would guess, the son was back in no time, asking again, "What holds up the elephant?" The frustrated father, having run out of animals, replied, "Son, from there on, it's elephants all the way down."

As we consider the Apostles' Creed, we are thinking together about the elephants that go all the way down to the bottom of our faith, the foundational affirmations upon which our lives and beliefs as Christian people rest, as they are described in the Apostles' Creed. Take one look at the creed, and you'll discover that it is ruthlessly trinitarian; it hangs on three central affirmations. First, we say, "I believe in God, the Father Almighty." Then we affirm, "I believe in Jesus Christ, his only Son, our Lord." Finally, we say, "I believe in the Holy Spirit." When we stand to affirm the creed, we are immediately thrown into the central mystery of the Christian faith: "God in three persons, blessed Trinity!"

Let's begin by acknowledging that the idea of the Trinity is a mystery. A preacher friend of mine told his congregation that the problem with the Trinity is that if you don't believe it you risk losing your soul, but if you try to explain it you risk losing your mind. We are attempting to comprehend the incomprehensible, to describe the indescribable. We are like the Sunday school student who was working intently with her crayons and paper when the teacher asked, "What are you drawing?" The student answered, "A picture of God." The teacher responded, "God? No one knows what God looks like." With childlike confidence the student said, "They will when I get done."

> *"The only way we know God is through God's self-revelation. A finite mind cannot wrap itself around an infinite God."*

Anyone who dares to speak of God must begin by acknowledging that all of our words about God are incomplete and that none of us dares to have the arrogance to think he or she can fully define the identity of God. In the sixteenth century, an Anglican mystic named Richard Hooker said, "Our safest eloquence concerning [God] is our silence"—a reminder that could put a whole lot of preachers out of business! Four centuries later, Karl Barth, a German theologian, reminded us that in and of our own human nature we do not even know what we are saying when we say the word *God*. The only way we know God is through God's self-revelation. A finite mind cannot wrap itself around an infinite God, just as my finite being cannot take in the full glory of a new morning, my eyes cannot absorb the full brightness of the sun, and my brain cannot comprehend the full meaning of love.

I cannot pin God down like a butterfly under a microscope and say, "There! Now I've got it!" Belief in the Trinity is not our attempt to say, "We've got God cornered. This pins God down." Rather, it is the response of the church to God's self-revelation in the creation (the Father), in history (Jesus of Nazareth), and in our present experience (the Holy Spirit). It is the formula by which we describe our experience of God, and it says two important things.

First, we affirm that there is one God. Biblical faith rests on a radical monotheism: "Hear, O Israel: The LORD is our God, the LORD alone. You shall love the LORD your God with your heart, and with all your soul, and with all your might" (Deut. 6:4-5). The biblical pilgrimage of faith revolves around this God, who says, "I am the LORD your God . . . you shall have no other gods before me" (Exod. 20:2-3).

> *"The dilemma of our times is not what it means to live without a god, but what it means to live with too many gods."*

When I began working on this sermon, I thought it would be a response to atheism, an attempt to explain why it makes sense to believe in God. But as I thought about this affirmation in the context of our contemporary world, I realized that the struggle we face is not with atheism, but with polytheism. The dilemma of our times is not what it means to live without a god, but what it means to live with too many gods—puny little gods who compete for our ultimate loyalty. To claim belief in the God of Abraham and Sarah, Isaac and Jacob, Moses and Jesus is to dethrone all of the trivial gods to which we so easily give our allegiance.

Some of us serve the gods of wealth, materialism, money, or greed. For us, to affirm the creed is to hear Jesus ask, "What shall it profit a person to gain the whole world but lose his or her soul?" Some of us worship the god of sex and hedonistic pleasure. For us to affirm belief in one God is to hear the word: "Do you not know that your body is a temple of the Holy Spirit within you, which you have from God, and that you are not your own? For you were bought with a price; therefore glorify God in your body" (I Cor. 6:19-20). Some of us follow the god of power. For us to affirm faith in the God revealed in the cross is to hear Jesus say, "Many who are first will be last, and the last will be first. . . . The greatest among you will be your servant" (Matt. 19:30; 23:11). Some of us salute the god of narrow, jingoistic, nationalistic pride. For us, to worship the God of the Bible is to hear the Spirit say, "God has made of one blood all nations to worship him" (Acts 17:26, paraphrased). To affirm that we believe in one God is to strip bare all the altars that we erect to lesser gods. It is to kneel before the God who says, "I, the LORD your God, am One. You shall have no other gods before me."

The second foundational affirmation is that God has been revealed to us in three persons. As followers of Jesus, we go into the world, commissioned in the name of the Father, the Son, and the Holy Spirit.

> *"The Christian faith affirms that the God who is . . . the one, almighty God is known to us in three primary relationships."*

I used to explain the Trinity by comparing it to water. Water is always composed of two parts hydrogen and one part oxygen. But it can be experienced in three different forms: a solid when it is ice, a liquid when it is water, and a gas when it evaporates. It's always water, but we experience it in three different ways. That's not bad, as analogies go, but I began to feel that the water analogy was too analytical, too objective, too cold, too distant. The story of Adam and Eve teaches us at the very beginning of the Bible that God is experienced in relationships. So I began to look for a relational image for the Trinity. It's a little like this: I am Jim Harnish. That's who I am, and that's who I'll always be. But I am experienced in three primary relationships: To my mother, I am a son; to my wife, I am a husband; to my daughters, I am a father—one person, experienced in three relationships.

The Christian faith affirms that the God who *is*, the God who created the planets and the universe, the God who gives life and breath to all that exists, the God who is the very ground of all being, the God who is the one, almighty God is known to us in three primary relationships. First, God is known to us as the creative parent, the God who in the fullness of parenthood conceives life, the source of all that is and all that ever shall be. Second, this eternal God has entered into our human experience as the Son, our elder brother, Jesus of Nazareth. In him we have experienced the living God in human terms. Third, this God is present with us as the Spirit, present in our fellowship, alive in our worship, taking up residence in our souls, and providentially at work in our world. One God, known in three primary relationships.

I know this is not an adequate explanation of the Trinity. It provides almost as many questions as answers, but it is at least a side door into the mystery of God's self-revelation. The critical factor is that the God we affirm in the creed is revealed to us in profoundly personal terms. The Trinity is our way of responding to the God who comes to us as Father, Son, and Holy Spirit.

The origin of the Apostles' Creed was in baptism in the early church, which is why it is included as a part of our new United Methodist liturgy for baptism. Early on Easter Sunday morning, the first Christians would wade, naked as they were at birth, into the water. They would be asked, "Do you believe in God the Father Almighty?" The candidates would respond, "I do," and under the water the candidates would go. Then they would be asked, "Do you believe in Jesus Christ, his only Son, our Lord?" They would respond, "I do," and under the water they'd go. Finally, the candidates would be asked, "Do you believe in the Holy Spirit?" They would say, "I do," and under the water they'd go. With each affirmation, the candidates would submerge themselves in water— experiencing the surrender of themselves, the purging, the cleansing of all other gods, the binding of themselves to this three-personed God. Each time they would rise from the water like newborn children from their mothers' wombs—their new identity shaped by their affirmation of faith.

That's still what it means to affirm this creed. When I stand in the congregation and say these ancient words, I am renewing my baptism, affirming my identity, pledging my loyalty, and offering myself anew in relationship with this God who comes to me in three persons. John Donne described the experience this way:

> Batter my heart, three personed God; for You
> As yet but knock, breathe, shine, and seek to mend. . . .
> Take me to You, imprison me, for I,
> Except You enthrall me, never shall be free,
> Nor ever chaste, except You ravish me.
>
> ("Holy Sonnet 14")

"... in God, the Father Almighty"

> *If you then, who are evil, know how to give good gifts to your children, how much more will your Father in heaven give good things to those who ask him! (Matt. 7:11)*

Do We Dare to Call God "Father"?

A little Roman Catholic boy surprised his parents by telling them that their Irish priest was God. When the parents asked how he had come to that conclusion, he replied, "Every day at mass we all stand up and say, 'I believe in God, the Father O'Malley.' "

That little boy was close. Every time we affirm the Apostles' Creed we identify the God in whom we believe as "the Father Almighty." But what does it mean for finite human beings to address the almighty God as "Father"?

While "Father" is the most common way Christians have described God, it also has become the most controversial way in the light of our growing concern for inclusive language. A recent denominational poll confirmed that while most members of that denomination have accepted inclusive language in addressing human beings—they would much rather say "Sing with All the *Saints* in Glory" than "Sing with All the *Sons* of Glory"—they are not ready to trade in the traditional terms of "Father" and "Son" for "Creator" and "Redeemer." It's more than language; the debate goes to the heart of our understanding of the identity of God. It has opened our eyes to see God in a multitude of new ways, to break free from male-dominated traditions to rediscover the biblical images of maternal as well as paternal love. For this sermon, however, let's take a fresh look at what it means to use the term *Father* in relationship to God.

> ## "The Bible does not say that God is male."

I pulled my concordance off the shelf and read through every verse in the Bible in which God is described as "Father." I discovered two things.

First, when the Bible calls God "Father," it is describing relationship, and not gender. The Bible does not say that God is male. In fact, the first thing we hear about God is that God created both male and female in God's own image. On the human side, being female is just as much a part of the image of God as being male. On the divine side, the God who is infinitely larger than any of our human categories relates to us in ways that we male and female human beings can comprehend. By calling God "Father," we are describing the profoundly personal relationship between an infinite God and finite beings like us.

The second discovery I made was that when the New Testament writers call God "Father," they are not speaking in an all-purpose, greeting-card sense. Neither are they talking about God as the source of all creation. They specifically describe God as "the father of our Lord Jesus Christ." God's fatherhood is defined by God's relationship with Jesus. When I discovered that, I immediately wanted to see what it meant for Jesus to call God "Father."

Let's begin with the only story the Gospel writers record of the boyhood of Jesus (Luke 2:41-52). Mary, Joseph, and the twelve-year-old Jesus go to Jerusalem for Passover. When the festival is over, Mary and Joseph start home, assuming that Jesus is with the other families. When evening comes, however, Jesus is nowhere to be found. Every parent can identify with their fear and frustration. They trace their steps back to the Temple and find him talking with the priests and teachers of the law.

Now that she knows he is safe, Mary's maternal fear turns to anger. "Why have you treated us like this?" she cries. And Jesus replies, "Did you not know that I must be in my Father's house?" (Luke 2:48-49).

Don't miss the fact that Jesus is twelve, right at the edge of the normal adolescent identity crisis, right at the point at which each of us asks, "Who am I? How do I define my identity? By what values will I live?" I imagine that Jesus' answer to those questions is "I will define my identity not primarily in relation to my biological, human ancestry, but in my relationship with God."

It makes a radical difference in how we understand our own identity if we begin by saying, "I have a heavenly Father, a divine parentage; I am not just a human animal. I am a child of God."

> *"Jesus is not saying that God is a Cosmic Santa Claus who gives us everything we want."*

Twenty-five years down the road, Matthew pictures Jesus teaching on a mountainside. The underlying theme of the Sermon on the Mount is simply this: You are not an orphan; you are the child of God, who relates to you as a loving parent. So trust yourself to God and live as if you wanted to be like him. Listen to Jesus' words:

> Why do you worry. . . ? Consider the lilies of the field, how they grow; they neither toil nor spin, yet I tell you, even Solomon in all his glory was not clothed like one of these. But if God so clothes the grass of the field, which is alive today and tomorrow is thrown into the oven, will he not much more clothe you—you of little faith? (Matt. 6:28-30)

If you then, who are evil, know how to give good gifts to your children, how much more will your Father in heaven give good things to those who ask him! (Matt. 7:11)

Jesus is not saying that God is a cosmic Santa Claus who gives us everything we want. Jesus is saying that God is the loving Parent who gives us everything we need. Because we can depend on the character of God, we are called to live that way ourselves. "Love your enemies and pray for those who persecute you, so that you may be children of your Father in heaven. . . . Be perfect, therefore, as your heavenly Father is perfect" (Matt. 5:44, 48).

Come now to the encroaching darkness of the Garden of Gethsemane (Matt. 26:36-46). When I began studying the references to God as Father, I did not expect them to lead me here. I was not ready to share the struggle in Jesus' soul as he wrestled with whether or not he would be obedient to the call of God. I did not want to hear him cry, "My Father, if it is possible, let this cup pass from me" (Matt. 26:39).

If you are a parent, have you ever heard that from your child? "Daddy, don't make me go to the dentist! Mama, don't make me take that medicine!" You know how that feels. Multiply that cry by the power of infinite compassion, and you will begin to be within reach of what it meant for Jesus to pray, "Father, let this cup pass from me.

If there is any way for the world to be saved without my going to the cross, let's find it!"

But the answer was no. There was no way for God to save the world and save his Son. The most profound mystery of the gospel is God's act of redemption in Jesus. So Jesus prays, "Father, if there is no other way, I will be obedient to your redemptive will, even if it means going to the cross. Your will be done"—not "your will" in the sense that God caused Jesus to suffer on the cross, but "your will" in that it is God's will that the world be made whole, and that wholeness can only be accomplished through the total identification of God with our humanity.

To claim that kind of God as my Father means that I, like Jesus, am willing to walk the road of obedience to God's love, regardless of the cost. It means that I, like Jesus, am willing to share the pain and suffering of the world, and thereby be a part of God's redemption. It means that I am willing, like Jesus, to face the awesome reality of death in the hope of new life.

> *"To call God 'Father' is to acknowledge my own need and to experience the amazing grace of a forgiving God."*

And so we walk with him to Golgotha, where we hear him pray, "Father, forgive them; for they do not know what they are doing" (Luke 23:34). To call God "Father" is to acknowledge my own need and to experience the amazing grace of a forgiving God.

We listen for Jesus' last breath when he prays, "Father, into your hands I commend my spirit" (Luke 23:46). With the absolute trust of a child resting in a parent's arms,

Jesus entrusts himself to the infinite care of God. To call God "Father" is to live with that kind of trust.

I believe in God, the Father Almighty. We dare not allow our familiarity with this statement to blind us to the depth of that affirmation. When we dare to call God "Father" the way Jesus called God "Father," we are drawn into the flow of divine love and challenge of costly discipleship. Are we ready for that?

"... creator of heaven and earth"

Where were you when I laid the foundation of the earth? (Job 38:4)

Creation Out of Chaos

Opening sentences are tough for me. I don't know whether it's true for every preacher, but I know it's true for me. I probably spend more time on the opening paragraph than any other single part of the sermon. If I can get that opening line right, the rest of the sermon will often fall into place. As opening lines go, this one is hard to beat: "In the beginning when God created the heavens and the earth, the earth was a formless void and darkness covered the face of the deep, while [the Spirit of] God swept over the face of the waters. Then God said, 'Let there be light'; and there was light" (Gen. 1:1-3).

It is, of course, the opening sentence of the book of Genesis, the opening paragraph in the Bible, the opening line in the drama of God's relationship with human history. Here's how *The Living Bible* paraphrases it: "When God began creating the heavens and the earth, the earth was at first a shapeless, chaotic mass, with the Spirit of God brooding over the dark vapors." It sounds like the screenplay for a Stephen Speilberg movie, doesn't it? Now, listen to this description:

When time began—perhaps as long as 20 billion years ago—all mass and energy were compressed almost to infinite density and heated to trillions upon trillions of degrees. A cosmic explosion rent that featureless mass, creating a rapidly expanding fireball. It has been cooling ever since. At first the universe was an impenetrable haze . . . the universe cleared and everywhere blazed with light.

It sounds like a paraphrase of Genesis, doesn't it? But it's not. It comes directly out of *National Geographic* (163, 6 [June 1983]: 704A).

> *"We believe that the Spirit of God is that creative power who rends the dark emptiness with light and brings into being all that is."*

One Friday at the men's breakfast, one of the guys, having noticed the title for that week's sermon, asked, "Jim, have you seen the latest issue of *National Geographic?*" I told him that it had arrived in the mail, but I hadn't opened it. He handed me his copy. The cover introduced a major article on "The Once and Future Universe," complete with a foldout chart of the "Journey Into the Universe Through Time and Space."

Though some of it was clearly beyond my comprehension, it impressed me that the magazine had printed the best of biblical faith and the best of scientific knowledge at exactly the same place, almost word for word.

National Geographic: "a featureless mass."
Genesis: "without form and void," "a shapeless, chaotic mass."
National Geographic: "an impenetrable haze."
Genesis: "The Spirit of God brooding over the dark, gaseous
    mass."

National Geographic: "the universe cleared and everywhere blazed with light."
Genesis: "God said, 'Let there be light' and there was
light."

Science and faith begin at the same place: meaningless,
chaotic nothingness. To stand up in worship and say "I
believe in God, the creator of heaven and earth" is to identify God as the creative force who brings creation out of
chaos, beauty out of barenness, light out of darkness, life
out of nothingness. We believe that the Spirit of God is
that creative power who rends the dark emptiness with
light and brings into being all that is.

*I believe in God, the Father Almighty, creator of heaven and
earth* is the beginning affirmation of our faith, the
ground-level assumption of the Christian life. But what
are the implications of that affirmation for our lives?
What difference does it make for us to say that God is the
creator of heaven and earth, the One who brings creation
out of chaos? First, this affirmation means that behind the
created order is a purposeful Creator—or, to turn it
around the other way, this created order, this infinite
expanse of galaxies stretching beyond galaxies, bears witness to its creator.

On a recent trip through Amsterdam, we spent a long
afternoon roaming through the Rijksmuseum, which
houses some of Rembrandt's greatest works, including the
massive "Nightwatch." You don't have to be an art authority to recognize Rembrandt's work; the fascinating use of
light and shadow, rich colors, and detailed faces point
beyond themselves to the artist who created them. A work
of art bears witness to the imagination, vision, and creative intent of the artist. Biblical faith looks at the created
universe from this perspective:

The heavens are telling the glory of God;
  and the firmament proclaims his handiwork. . . .
There is no speech, nor are there words;
  their voice is not heard;
yet their voice goes out through all the earth,
  and their words to the end of the world. (Ps. 19:1, 3-4)

After the men's breakfast that Friday morning, I talked at length with the man who told me about the *National Geographic* article. A retired scientist, he was fascinated with the article, the research behind it, and the age and magnitude of the universe. But most of all, he was fascinated by the capacity of the human mind to think, study, and pursue understanding to the edge of infinity. I still remember the sense of awe in his voice when he said, "There must be a God, to give human beings minds that can begin to perceive the process of creation!"

> *"To believe in God as the maker of heaven and earth is to celebrate that mystery and to live with a sense of awe and wonder."*

That's biblical faith. The Bible is not a science book, which tries to analyze the creation under a microscope; it is a book of faith that celebrates the power and the purpose of the Creator. The more we expand our understanding, the more we stretch our minds to comprehend the processes of creation, the larger our faith can become in the God who is the creative power at work in the universe.

Lest we become enamored of our own intelligence, we must go on to say that to believe that God is the maker of heaven and earth is to acknowledge our own limitations as a part of the creation. We are finite, human, bound by time and space, incomplete in our comprehension of the creation and the creator. The tiny amount we know is surrounded by the infinite mystery we can never fully comprehend. To believe in God as the maker of heaven and earth is to celebrate that mystery and to live with a sense of awe and wonder.

Do you remember how Job struggled with this? In the middle of his suffering, his well-intentioned, intelligent friends use all their human wisdom, all of their powers of logic and debate to try to explain the ways of God. After they have done their best and their worst, God finally comes onto the stage. And when God speaks, it is with high satire and profound irony.

> Where were you when I laid the
>   foundation of the earth?
> Tell me, if you have understanding
> Who determined its measurements—surely you know!
>   Or who stretched the line upon it? . . .
> When the morning stars sang together,
>   and all the heavenly beings shouted for joy. . . .
> Have you commanded the morning since your days began?
>   and caused the dawn to know its place? . . .
> Have you comprehended the expanse of the earth? . . .
> Shall a faultfinder contend with the Almighty?
>   Anyone who argues with God must respond.
>   (Job 38:4-5, 7, 12-13, 18; 40:1-2)

Job responds out of profound trust and faith:

> See, I am of small account; what shall I answer you?
>   I lay my hand on my mouth.
> I have spoken once, and I will not answer.
>   (Job 40:4-5)

There are times when the most eloquent expression of faith is silence. To live by faith is to live with that sense of awe and wonder that stands in silence before the greatness of creation, to dance with the music that could only be heard at the dawn of creation.

When it comes down to it, I have problems with both extremes of the creationism debate; the totally secular scientists and the religious fundamentalists are both too sure of themselves. Both hike up their absolute answers like hip boots and stomp on the mystery. Genuine biblical faith acknowledges that we are human, that our understanding is incomplete. We celebrate the mystery of the creation.

> *"God's creative work goes on, and by the power of the Spirit of God, you and I are invited to be a part of it."*

The *National Geographic* article said that the universe will keep on expanding indefinitely. As far as science can tell, the process keeps going on. And that's a part of our faith, too. The creative Spirit who brooded over the nothingness of chaos continues to be at work to accomplish God's creative purpose in the world today. The Apostle Paul said, "Anyone who is in Christ becomes a whole new creation. The old has passed away, the new has come" (II Cor. 5:17, paraphrased). God's creative work goes on, and by the power of the Spirit of God, you and I are invited to be a part of it.

There is a profoundly practical implication to that affirmation. Like a sculptor who places his or her prized work of art in our hands, God has entrusted us with the care of the created order. People of biblical faith are incorrigible environmentalists because we believe that this earth, the planets, and this universe are physical expressions of God's creative intent, entrusted to our care.

There is also a profoundly personal implication to the affirmation that we are invited to be a part of God's creative work. When I look at my own life and the life of the world around me, I know that I don't have to reach any farther than my own soul to experience chaos. Within my arm's reach are persons who experience disorder, confusion, and nothingness. We all need that creative Spirit who brings order and harmony out of the chaos and disorder of life. Controlled by the Spirit of God, we become part of the new creation, bringing order and wholeness to the life of our world.

I believe—which means I trust, I love, I give myself to—*in God, the Father Almighty, creator of heaven and earth.*

Let us pray:

God, who touchest earth with beauty, Make me lovely, too;
With Thy Spirit recreate me, Make my heart anew.
Like the springs and running waters, Make me crystal pure.
Like the rocks of towering grandeur, Make me strong and
    sure.
Like Thy dancing waves in sunlight, Make me glad and free;
Like the straightness of the pine tree, Let me upright be.
Like the arching of the heavens, Lift my thought above;
Turn my dreams to noble action—Ministries of love.
(M. S. Edgar, "God Who Touchest Earth with Beauty")

"Jesus Christ, his only Son . . . "

> *But in these last days he has spoken to us by a Son, whom he appointed heir of all things, through whom he also created the worlds.*
> *(Heb. 1:2)*

How Human Is Your God?

A fascinating exhibit that opened at the Boston Museum of Science in 1987 has been making its way around the major cities of the nation for the past several years. "Robots and Beyond" is described as "a futuristic carnival" in which more than three dozen displays present the latest accomplishments in machines that act like people. I was particularly interested in the *Time* magazine description of a clear plastic manikin with artificial "skin." This skin is actually a piezoelectric film that transforms physical pressure into electrical impulses—like the kind of thing you touch on the front of your microwave. "When visitors touch the manikin's chest, electrical signals activate a computer voice system programmed to interpret different types of touch. Gentle pressure may elicit a languid, 'Oooh, I can feel that.' But a rapid-fire tap prompts, 'Hey! Cut it out! What are you, a woodpecker?' But, of course, it can't feel anything. No matter how real the manikin looks on the outside, on the inside it is nothing but electric currents, wires, plastic, and a computerized voice. There is not a drop of blood in it.

No matter what it says, it is incapable of feeling love or fear, of celebrating human emotions, or of comprehending joy or pain. In the end, Jorel, a robot in the exhibition, concedes, "You humans are marvelous!" (" 'Ouch! Oooh! Cut It Out!' " *Time* [February 9, 1987]: 78).

> " . . . *the astounding claim of the Christian gospel is that the eternal God . . . is also the God who has become one of us.*"

To hear some folks talk about God, you might get the impression that the divine being is like those fascinating robots: a perfectly coordinated machine that is capable of acting or looking like a human being, but that certainly is not a god who feels human passion, pain, suffering, and joy. God is "the unmoved mover," or "the ground of all being," or "the first cause." There is truth in each of these terms. But the astounding claim of the Christian gospel is that the eternal God, the God of creation, the God of history, the God who is the source of all things, is also the God who has become one of us, the God who has visited human history in human form. John says God, the Eternal Word through which creation came into being, "became flesh and dwelt among us." The writer of the letter to the Hebrews describes it this way: "God spoke to our ancestors in many and various ways by the prophets, but in these last days he has spoken to us by a Son. . . . He is the reflection of God's glory and the exact imprint of God's very being" (Heb. 1:1-3).

The creed drives the affirmation home with words that graphically describe the human experience: *conceived, born, suffered, died, was buried.* It's the story of your life and mine, from our conception to our death. In the human life of Jesus of Nazareth, the eternal God has felt our pain, shared our joy, experienced our sorrow, entered our suffering, and gone with us to death. This Jesus is Immanuel, God with us, the eternal God in human skin.

This astounding affirmation is, of course, open to infinite theoretical debate. But rather than enter into the rarefied air of philosophical discussion, let's begin with the affirmation and ask what practical difference it makes in our lives if we actually believe it to be true.

> *"Through Jesus we know, more fully than we have ever known before, who God is."*

First, to affirm that Jesus is God's Son means that through Jesus we know something about God. We have felt the heartbeat at the center of the universe; we have heard the voice of the infinite God; we have seen the personality of the divine being. "God, the one who in fragmentary and diverse ways communicated his purpose and character through the prophets, has now spoken through a Son. Jesus bears the stamp of the nature of God" (Heb. 1:1-3, paraphrased).

Several years ago I read an article in *The New Yorker* in which Brendon Gill, a New York theater critic, bemoaned the way that all of the Broadway musicals are now miked and amplified. He noted that in grand old theaters, where actors had spoken and sung with ease for half a century, audiences are now obliged to listen to what he called a "totally phony sound." He complained that "the voice is never heard in its ordinary resonance."

45

In contrast, I have a friend who sings in an Italian restaurant. Without amplification, and often without accompaniment, she steps into the center of the dining room, walks around the tables, and with the "ordinary resonance" of her human voice, she soars into the masterpieces of Italian opera. The naked power of her voice is so real, so genuine, so human that you can almost touch it.

The gospel is the story of the God who was not satisfied with sending his word through messengers in fragmentary and partial ways. The day came when God's voice was heard through the cry of a baby bursting from Mary's womb, through the laughter of friendship along the seashore, through the cry of sorrow beside the grave of a friend, through a shuddering scream in the hour of death. God has spoken through the sheer, naked power of human experience. Through Jesus we know, more fully than we have ever known before, who God is.

> *"In the human Jesus, God stepped onto the stage of human history, sat down among us, and found out how it feels."*

The second implication of the affirmation that Jesus is God's Son is that God knows who we are. In 1950, the story goes, Charlie Chaplin directed a play at the Circle Theatre in Hollywood. During one of the rehearsals he became frustrated with how things were going on the stage. To the surprise of all the actors, the director leapt out of his seat, jumped onto the stage, pushed one of the actors off a chair, sat down, and said, "Excuse me, please, I want to sit here for a while. I need to see how it feels."

The writer of the letter to the Hebrews makes a daring claim when he describes Jesus as our "High Priest" who has gone for us into the heavenly presence of God: "We have not an high priest which cannot be touched with the feeling of our infirmities; but was in all points tempted like as we are, yet without sin" (Heb. 4:15 KJV). Turn the negatives around, and it would read, "We *have* a high priest who *is touched* by the feelings of our infirmities." God is not some distant celestial robot. In the human Jesus, God stepped onto the stage of human history, sat down among us, and found out *how it feels.*

We may question the way God put the universe together, with all of its hurts and disappointments, its weakness, pain, sorrow, and death, but one thing we must say about God is that God was willing to take this life the way we take it. God was willing to play by the same rules we do: *conceived, born, suffered, died,* and *buried.*

There is a phrase in the older versions of the Apostles' Creed that has been omitted by most of the Protestant churches. The statement "He descended into hell" was removed or placed in a footnote by many denominations because there is scant biblical witness for it. It may or may not be biblically accurate, but to many it has significant meaning. I have a psychologist friend who described his work with patients in a mental health hospital. They were planning a worship service, and when they came to a discussion of the creed, the patients insisted that the phrase be left in. To them it meant that Jesus had descended into their own experience of hell and was present with them. God knows the feelings of our human infirmities. Because of Jesus, God knows something about us.

In her musical revue entitled *For Heaven's Sake,* Helen Kromer summed up the effect that the affirmation that Jesus is God's Son has on an individual life.

I'm nothing, I'm nobody, no one,
I'm something in Christ who's in me;
And I'll put on His flesh
And I'll walk in His bones
And a part of His body I'll be!
  (Helen L. Kromer, *For Heaven's Sake*)

"Jesus Christ . . . Our Lord"

He said to [the disciples], "But who do you say that I am?" Simon Peter answered, "You are the Messiah, the Son of the living God."
(Matt. 16:15-16)

Who Do You Say He Is?

I t was one of those brief, shining moments, bristling with excitement and expectation. Jesus and the disciples were on their way to Jerusalem. As faithful Jews had experienced it for generations, they too felt the anticipation rising as they made their way toward the Holy City—like the excitement children (and adults!) feel on their way to Walt Disney's Magic Kingdom. On the way through Caesarea Philippi, they stopped for a picnic lunch. During their meal, Jesus asked them: "Who do the people say that I am?"

The disciples had been listening to the crowds in the streets, the chatter around the wells, the gossip over the garden wall. They all had something to report. "Some say you are John the Baptist, returned from the dead." "Some say you are Elijah." "I heard some say they thought you were Jeremiah or one of the prophets." Jesus listened, and then looked them straight in the eyes with a penetrating gaze that went to the center of their souls as he asked, "But what about you? Who do *you* say that I am?"

Suddenly things became very quiet. No one would even take a bite. It was the unnerving kind of silence that drowns out every other sound when we find ourselves pinned to the wall, when we can no longer report what others are saying but must finally speak up for ourselves.

The disciples squirmed, avoiding one another's eyes, dragging their toes in the sand, hoping that someone would break the frightening silence. Finally, to no one's surprise and everyone's relief, Peter did it. Hardly aware of the full weight of what he was saying, he blurted out the most honest answer he could give: "You are the Christ, the Son of the living God!" From somewhere deep within his soul, from a place deeper than conscious thought, there came this response of loyalty and commitment: "Whoever you are to everyone else, whatever anyone else may say about you, to me you are the chosen One of God, the Messiah, the Lord!"

> *"The Jesus who shares our humanity all the way to death is also the Jesus who gives us hope of eternal life."*

I will always remember one of the first baptisms in my first pastoral appointment. The child being baptized was the infant son of a prominent surgeon in the community. The relatives were all there, prim and proper, attempting to live up to the expected dignity of the moment. The time came for the question, "What name shall be given this child?" Before the father could respond with the full name, the baby's preschool-aged sister shouted, "That's Jimmy!" It did not matter what anyone else said, she knew who that child was! Others could call him anything they liked, but to her he was Jimmy. Something like that must have happened to Peter that day. He simply knew that Jesus was the Christ, the Son of the living God, and, therefore, his Lord.

The Apostles' Creed describes Jesus from two perspectives. First, the Creed describes Jesus as God's Son. That's objective. But the creed also identifies Jesus as our Lord, which is our subjective response to his life, teaching, death, and resurrection.

We have thought about how God has identified with us in Jesus: *conceived, born, suffered, died, buried.* But that is not the end of the story. "The third day he rose from the dead." The Jesus who shares our humanity all the way to death is also the Jesus who gives us hope of eternal life.

> *"The cross and resurrection are the focal points of the Christian faith, the ultimate fulfillment of the Christ event."*

Novelist John Irving has probed the depths of religious experience in his best-selling novel *A Prayer for Owen Meany.* Walking home from worship on Palm Sunday, the narrator reflects on the meaning of Holy Week and remembers Owen Meany's profound faith in the resurrection.

I find that Holy Week is draining; no matter how many times I have lived through his crucifixion, my anxiety about his resurrection is undiminished—I am terrified that, this year, it won't happen; that, that year, it didn't. Anyone can be sentimental about the Nativity; any fool can feel like a Christian at Christmas. But Easter is the main event; if you don't believe in the resurrection, you're not a believer.

"IF YOU DON'T BELIEVE IN EASTER," Owen Meany said, "DON'T KID YOURSELF—DON'T CALL YOURSELF A CHRISTIAN."

Easter is the main event. The cross and resurrection are the focal points of Christian faith, the ultimate fulfillment of the Christ event. Peter was called to make his response of faith solely on the basis of the teachings and ministry of Jesus. You and I are invited to make ours in the light of the completed story, the full drama of the cross and the resurrection. On the basis of all of this, who do you say Jesus is?

There are only a few alternatives open to us. One possibility is that Jesus was sincere, but psychotic, deranged, out of touch with reality. Mental hospitals are full of people who think they are God. Most of them are sincere in their belief, but they are also crazy. But when you read Jesus' words, when you look at his life, when you see his influence in the world, does this seem to you to be the stuff of a madman? Is it not exactly the opposite? Doesn't a lot of what we call sanity seem to be insanity and a lot of what we call order seem to be disorder before the simplicity, the honesty, and the integrity of his life? And do the people who have believed in him—not the religious carnival barkers and sideshow fanatics, but the best of them—seem crazy to you?

A second possibility is that he was an impostor who deliberately deceived the people around him, and that his followers have continued the deception for nearly two thousand years. During my college days a book entitled *The Passover Plot* created quite a stir as it set out to prove that Jesus had not really died on the cross but that it was all a carefully conceived plot. One of the problems with the book was that the author insisted on the basic goodness of Jesus, which forced me to wonder: Could a man who denounced hypocrisy be an impostor and still be good?

A third possibility is that Jesus was and is exactly who the creed says he is: nothing more or less than the Son of God. This means that he is God present with us in human form. He was conceived, born, suffered, and died like all of us; however, on the third day he rose again, ascended into heaven, and now sits at the right hand of God. Jesus is, therefore, the moral, ethical, and spiritual standard by which all life and reality are measured.

> *"The affirmation of the lordship of Christ is the human response to his life, death, and resurrection. It is our human response to our personal experience."*

If we take the first option—that Jesus was sincere but psychotic—we can pity him. If we take the second—that he was an impostor—we can reject him. But if the third option is true, the only appropriate response is to call him Lord—lord of our lives and lord of human history. C. S. Lewis came to this conclusion in his classic *Mere Christianity*.

A man who was merely a man and said the sort of things Jesus said would not be a great moral teacher. He would either be a lunatic—on a level with a man who says he is a poached egg—or else he would be the Devil from Hell. You must make your choice. Either this man was, and is, the Son of God: or else a madman or something worse. You can shut him up for a fool, you can spit at him and kill him as a demon; or you can fall at his feet and call him Lord and God. But let us not come with any patronizing nonsense about his being a great human teacher. He has not left that open to us. He did not intend to. (C. S. Lewis, *Mere Christianity,* book II [New York: Macmillan, 1964])

The earliest affirmation of faith for the Christian movement was three simple words: Jesus is Lord. Jesus is the one with undisputed authority over my values, my relationships, my time, my money, my home, my talents, and my world. Jesus is Lord.

The fascinating thing about this affirmation is that Jesus never imposes it, never forces it, never directly claims it for himself. Rather, the affirmation of the lordship of Christ is the human response to his life, death, and resurrection. It is our human response to our personal experience of God in Jesus of Nazareth.

That's how it was for Peter. The question was asked: "Who do you say I am?" And Peter responded, "You are the Christ, the Son of the living God." And that's how it is for us. The living Spirit of Christ meets us along the path of our lives and asks, "Who do you say I am?" How will you respond?

"He ascended into heaven"

> *[Christ] is the image of the invisible God, the firstborn of all creation. (Col. 1:15)*

The Cosmic Christic

Luke records: "They were gazing up toward heaven" (Acts 1:10). Through the spring and summer of 1990 we all had our eyes fixed on the sky, sharing the fascination and frustration of the Hubble Space Telescope.

I confess that the technology is beyond me. I haven't the faintest idea how NASA got that thing up there. All I know is that it will enable us to see farther and more clearly than we have ever seen before because it is beyond the fog of the earth's atmosphere. When it was launched, one science reporter promised that the Hubble Space Telescope would give us a whole new understanding of our own existence.

> *"Men and women of faith have discovered that . . . when they catch a vision of the crucified Jesus as their ascended Lord, they . . . discover a whole new understanding of their own existence."*

That is exactly where we find the first disciples in this final scene in the story of Jesus, with their eyes fixed on

55

the sky. According to Luke, Jesus was "lifted up, and a cloud took him out of their sight" (Acts 1:9).

I haven't the faintest idea how it happened. The astrophysics of the ascension are beyond me. I do not understand it any better than I understand the Hubble Space Telescope. I haven't the foggiest idea what literally happened on the mountaintop that day. But the church has never worried very much about that. Men and women of faith have discovered that when they lift their eyes toward the sky, when they catch a vision of the crucified Jesus as their ascended Lord, they are enabled to see farther and more clearly than they have ever seen before. In fact, they discover a whole new understanding of their own existence. They discover a whole new understanding of Christ.

It goes without saying that we no longer live with a Ptolemaic cosmology, which assumes that the earth is the central body around which the rest of the planets revolve. The words *up* and *down* have very different meanings for us than they did in 33 C.E. Yet, we still use this kind of language all the time. We talk about the sun rising and setting, though we know it does nothing of the kind. We describe a person who is on the way up, climbing the ladder, rising to the occasion. We say that one person is "up," or "on top of things," in contrast to another who is "down" or "depressed," for whom everything is going "downhill."

> *"The ascension, then, is the visual expression—the technicolor image—of faith in the cosmic Christ."*

We can still identify with the imagery and know what the biblical writers meant when they envisioned heaven—up, above, and beyond earthly realities—as that sphere where God's full purpose is accomplished, where all goodness, all power, and all life and wholeness are bound together. We know what those writers meant when they pictured Christ as coming down from God, descending to be with us in our humanity. God's presence in Christ descends into our suffering, our loneliness, our sorrow, walking with us into the darkness of injustice, violence, sin, and death. And so, at the end of the story, what else can we say? He was "taken up," back into the fullness and the wholeness of God. The cycle is complete, the circle is made whole. To conclude the story with Christ's ascending back to God is to say that what we have seen, heard, and experienced in the life, death, and resurrection of Jesus of Nazareth is infinitely more than the colorful recollection of a Hebrew rabbi peddling parables along the seashore and on the mountainsides of Palestine. What we have here is infinitely more than the tragic tale of a martyred Messiah who got caught on the wrong side of the power structures of his day and suffered the rejection and persecution of his people. What we have here is something of the cosmic drama of God's relationship with the creation.

The ascension is the visual expression of the most astonishing affirmation recorded in the New Testament:

[Christ] is the image of the invisible God, the firstborn of all creation; for in him all things in heaven and on earth were created . . . all things have been created through him and for him. He himself is before all things, and in him all things hold together. . . . In him all the fullness of God was pleased to dwell, and through him God was pleased to reconcile to himself all things. (Col. 1:15-20)

The ascension, then, is the visual expression—the technicolor image—of faith in the cosmic Christ.

Two friends helped to prepare me for this sermon. Over a year ago, a friend loaned me a copy of Stephen W. Hawking's best seller *A Brief History of Time: From the Big Bang to Black Holes.* I don't understand all of the book; some of it is as far beyond me as the Hubble Space Telescope. But I understand his conclusion: "We live in a bewildering world. We want to make sense of what we see around us." In his closing sentence, he says that the "ultimate triumph of human reason" will be "to know the mind of God." The other friend had many questions about "new age" ideas. What if this earth, with its time and space, is just a momentary blip in a cosmic process of evolution, constantly expanding, universe into universe, into infinity? Where does Christian faith fit in with that kind of vision of the cosmos?

I was working on this text at the time. As I wrestled with the conversation and thought about Hawking's book, I rediscovered what it means for people of faith to say—and it is a faith statement—that behind all of the cosmos, behind and beyond whatever worlds there are or ever will be, behind and through all that finds existence, there is an infinite, invisible, inexhaustible presence that we call God. This infinitely inexpressible God has chosen to reveal the essence of God's identity to us in a form that we human beings in this particular corner of time and space on this particular planet can comprehend. In Jesus of Nazareth we have seen the human likeness of the infinite God. The mind, the character, and the personality of the infinite God is the self-giving love that we see in the human form in Jesus of Nazareth.

I would like to paraphrase Paul's words: "Jesus of Nazareth is the visible, human likeness of the infinite, invisible, self-giving love of God. . . . God created the whole universe through and for that self-giving love. The love of God existed before all things. It is the cosmic glue which holds everything together. And through that self-sacrificing, life-producing love, God is at work to bring everything back together again" (Col. 1:15-20, paraphrased).

Now, if that sails over our heads, up into the rafters and out through the clerestory windows, we've probably gotten the point. The story of the ascension challenges our limited views of Christ. It lifts our eyes beyond the tunnel vision of our one-storied, flattened, ranch-style universe to see the love of God in cosmic terms. It stretches our minds, expands our souls, and lifts our vision. It enables us to see farther than we have ever seen before and gives us a whole new understanding of Christ.

> *"The church dares to affirm, dares to believe, dares to invite each of us to live as if ordinary folks like us are called and empowered to be the continuation of the self-giving love of Christ in the world."*

The ascension story also gives us a whole new understanding of ourselves. The most astonishing thing to me about the following passage from Acts is not what it says about Jesus, but what Jesus says about us: "You will receive power when the Holy Spirit has come upon you; and you will be my witnesses in Jerusalem, in all Judea and Samaria, and to the ends of the earth" (Acts 1:8). The church dares to affirm, dares to believe, dares to invite each of us to live as if ordinary folks like us are called and empowered to be the continuation of the self-giving love of Christ in the world. Ordinary folks like us are the extension of the life of Christ through his body, his hands, and his feet in the church. Folks like us are empowered by God's Spirit to be the visible likeness of the invisible Christ in our own time and our own place. We are the visible likeness of the invisible Christ! That's probably enough to shock any of us.

I know almost as little about opera as I do about the Hubble Space Telescope, but I know enough to recognize the name of Giacomo Puccini as one of the greatest composers of Italian opera. He began his last opera, *Turandot*, as he was dying of cancer, and he died before it was completed. There is a legend that one of his last words to a student was, "Remember *Turandot*." After his death, the opera was completed, and its premiere performance was on April 25, 1926, at La Scala in Milan. Arturo Toscanini, the greatest conductor of the time and one of Puccini's students, was on the podium. At the end of the first scene in the third act, Toscanini abruptly halted the performance, laid down his baton, turned to the audience with tears streaming down his face, and said, "At this point the maestro died." There was a moment of stunned silence. Then, triumphantly, he picked up the baton and said, "But his students have completed his work." And the opera went on.

We dare to believe that we are called to complete the work of our risen Lord in this world. The ascension is not the end of the life of Jesus but is the beginning of the life of the church. Paul says, "He is the head of his body, the church; he is the beginning" (Col. 1:18). It makes a huge difference in how we understand ourselves if we believe that we have been called to be the continuation of the self-giving love of God, witnesses to the cosmic Christ.

It may be that to fully experience the ascension story we have to see it from the underside of life. The book of Acts is the story of Christians who were struggling to survive through persecution and suffering. The letter to the Colossians was written to Christians who were attempting to maintain their identity in a pagan world. Perhaps to know the power of the ascension we have to lift our eyes out of the dark night of our own souls toward a dawn that we see faintly on the horizon. Perhaps we have to reach with some struggling hand of faith toward heaven because it feels for all the world as if we are living in hell. To persons on the underside of life, the word of the ascension comes as very good news.

If you have read William Faulkner's novel *The Sound and the Fury* you probably remember Dilsey, the courageous, faithful black woman who stands like a towering rock of strength through the decay and disintegration of the Compson family. One Sunday morning the old black preacher lifts the eyes of his poor, suffering congregation up out of the darkness to see the glory of the ascended Christ. Faulkner describes what happens to Dilsey:

> In the midst of the voices and the hands . . . Dilsey sat bolt upright . . . crying rigidly and quietly in the annealment and the blood of the remembered Lamb.
>
> As they walked through the bright noon, up the sandy road with the dispersing congregation talking easily again group to group, she continued to weep, unmindful of the talk. . . .
>
> Dilsey made no sound, her face did not quiver as the tears took their sunken and devious courses, walking with her head up, making no effort to dry them away even.
>
> "Whyn't you quit dat, mammy?" Frony said. "Wid all dese people lookin. We be passin white folks soon."
>
> "I've seed de first en de last," Dilsey said. "Never you mind me. . . . I seed de beginnin, en now I sees de endin."
> *The Sound and the Fury* [New York: Random House, 1984], p. 297)

When Faulkner described his characters, he used two words for Dilsey: "She endured."

I do not understand the ascension any more than I understand the Hubble Space Telescope. But I know that when we catch a vision of the ascended Christ we can see farther and more clearly than we have ever seen before, and it gives us a whole new way of understanding our own existence.

"I believe in the Holy Spirit"

> *If you love me, you will keep my commandments. And I will ask the Father, and he will give you another [Helper], to be with you forever. (John 14:15-16)*

The Helper Is on the Way

I t would be an understatement to say that in the winter of 1778 things were going poorly for the ragtag army led by General George Washington. The book makers were putting their bets on the British, who were feasting in Philadelphia while the American revolutionaries were freezing in Valley Forge. The event that turned the tide occurred on the other side of the Atlantic in Paris, on February 6, 1778, when Silas Dean and his team of negotiators worked out a treaty of alliance between the fledgling United States of America and France. Communication being what it was—they didn't have a FAX!—it took three months for the document to cross the ocean. It arrived in York, Pennsylvania, on May 2, 1778, where it was placed in the hands of the Continental Congress, who approved it on May 4, and one day later it reached General Washington. Recognizing the importance of the alliance, Washington declared May 6 a day of celebration. In those early years of our history, it ranked right up there with July 4. Listen to part of Washington's proclamation.

It having pleased the Almighty Ruler of the Universe propitiously to defend the cause of the United States of America and finally by raising us up a powerful friend, among the Princes of the Earth, to Establish Our Liberty and Independence upon lasting foundations; it becomes us to set apart a day, for fully acknowledging the Divine Goodness, and celebrating the important event which we owe to his Benign interposition. (Garrison Webb, *Sidelights on the American Revolution* [Nashville: Abingdon Press, 1974])

Were it not for the assistance of a "powerful friend," the American cause might easily have been lost, and today we would be singing "God Save the Queen."

In the fascinating twists of history, the time came when Winston Churchill called upon the United States to be that same kind of "powerful friend" for the British as they held the line against Hitler in World War II. Often the victory—and sometimes our survival—depends on receiving help from a powerful friend.

> *"Jesus promises a Helper, a powerful Friend, who is none other than the Spirit of God."*

With this image in mind, come back with me to an upper room in the city of Jerusalem, where Jesus' disciples gathered to celebrate the Passover. The writer of the fourth Gospel sets the scene in somber shades of pathos and human emotion. He tells us that Jesus knew it was his time to leave, and "having loved his own who were in the world, he loved them to the end" (John 13:1). The narrative is cloaked in the shroud of defeat, the darkness of despair, the shattering pain of separation and death. But in that darkness, Jesus' face shines with light, glowing like the central figure in a masterpiece painting: "I will ask the Father, and he will give you another Advocate, to be with you forever. . . . I will not leave you orphaned. . . . But the Advocate, the Holy Spirit, whom the Father will send in my name" (John 14:16, 18, 26).

Translators have struggled to find an appropriate word to capture the meaning of the Greek word *paraclete.* Some use *comforter,* which is fine if you lay aside memories of the soft, downy comforter on your grandmother's bed and remember that the root meaning of the word is "with strength." Others have used *advocate,* lifting the term out of its origin in the courts, where the "paraclete" would stand up for the accused. But when we get down to where we really live, it's hard to beat the identification of the Holy Spirit as the "helper." Jesus promises a Helper, a powerful Friend, who is none other than the Spirit of God.

The same Spirit who brooded over the chaos of nothingness and brought forth creation; the same Spirit who led the people of Israel out of Egyptian bondage; the same Spirit who healed the sick and liberated the oppressed through the ministry of Jesus; the same Spirit who strengthened Jesus in Gethsemane; the same Spirit who raised Jesus from death; the same Spirit who invaded the lives of the first disciples on Pentecost; the living, loving, laughing, life-giving Spirit of God that we saw in Jesus is now our Helper, our powerful Friend. In the hour of darkness, under the shadow of death, when it feels for all the world as if we are going down for the last time, isn't it good to know that we are not alone, that the Helper is on the way?

I am both fascinated and frustrated with the "doom and gloom" Christians who are constantly warning us that *the end* is near. Listen to some of them, and you will get the idea that the world has fallen so far, things have become so bad, that about all we can do is hold on for the downhill slide and wait for God to shut down the roller coaster. This is the religion of the helpless and hopeless, of those who feel that there is nothing they can do but prepare for the worse. But that is not the way Jesus tells his disciples to live.

> *"In the crucible of suffering we hear the sound of laughter, the song of gladness, the voice of hope, because we know that Christ has overcome the power of evil and is present with us through the Holy Spirit."*

Try to put yourself in the place of the first readers of this Gospel. Try to imagine how it felt to live under the oppressive heel of Roman occupation, with all the power of the emperor stacked up against you, the hungry lions growling for their dinner in the arena. Imagine how it felt to be politically and economically powerless, shut out because you refused to say, "Caesar is lord." Imagine what it is like to have no legal right of appeal, no freedom of speech, no recourse from the fury of armed might. Imagine how it feels to be black and live under apartheid or to be white and stand in protest of the emergency restrictions in South Africa. Imagine how it feels to stand alone in front of a tank in China, or to stand in solidarity with the oppressed poor in South America. If you can put yourself in those conditions, you can understand the realism of Jesus' words: "If the world hates you, be aware that it hated me before it hated you. . . . If they persecuted me, they will persecute you. . . . In the world you face persecution" (John 15:18, 20; 16:33).

That's realism; that's just how this world is. For the first followers of Jesus, the phrase "comfortable Christian" would have been an oxymoron, a contradiction of terms. Given the circumstances, you might expect this Gospel to be filled will gloom and doom. But listen to this: "You will have pain, but your pain will turn into joy. . . . I will see you again, and your hearts will rejoice, and no one will take your joy from you. . . . In the world you face persecution. But take courage; I have conquered the world!" (John 16:20, 22, 33). I still love the King James Version's translation of that last verse: "Be of good cheer; I have overcome the world."

There's no denying the tough realities of human experience, no avoiding the pain of suffering, no hiding from the persecution. But in the crucible of suffering we hear the sound of laughter, the song of gladness, the voice of hope, because we know that Christ has overcome the power of evil and is present with us through the Holy Spirit. The Helper comes to empower us to live victoriously in this world, not to help us pack our bags for the next world. The Holy Spirit is Christ present among us, saying, "Be of good cheer! I have overcome the world."

> *"The miracle of grace is that the Helper helps us in our own trouble when we help others in theirs."*

In his letter to the church in Corinth, Paul describes the way we experience the help of God:

Let us give thanks to the God and Father of our Lord Jesus Christ . . . the God from whom all help comes! He helps us

in all our troubles, so that we are able to help others who
have all kinds of troubles, using the same help that we ourselves have received from God. Just as we have a share in
Christ's many sufferings, so also through Christ we share in
God's great help. . . . We know that just as you share in our
sufferings, you also share in the help we receive. (II Cor.
1:3-5, 7 GNB)

Paul describes a marvelous chain reaction in which we
receive God's help in our trouble and are enabled to help
others with the same kind of help we receive. But this help
comes only to those who share in the suffering of others.
The miracle of grace is that the Helper helps us in our
own trouble when we help others in theirs.

In the summer of 1990 I had the privilege of sharing in
the ministry of Central Methodist Mission in downtown
Johannesburg, South Africa. I visited and worked with
men and women whose faith has been forged in the fur-
nace of apartheid, people who have faced detention,
imprisonment, ridicule, and persecution because of their
prophetic stand for justice, equality, and non-violence.
They were black Christians who have suffered the violence
of racism and white Christians who have entered into the
suffering of the black people around them. They continue
to face very difficult times. But when I remember their
faces, I see their smiles. When I listen for their voices, I
hear laughter as well as tears.

When you visit with people like these you find yourself
asking, "Why are they smiling? Where do they find such
joy?" The answer is clear: Their joy comes from the same
place as their pain; it comes in knowing that suffering
can result in new life. Their laughter emerges from the
same place as their tears. Their gladness is found only
through sorrow—it is, Jesus said, the kind of gladness a
woman feels when she experiences the very real pain of
childbirth (John 16:21)—and this gladness comes in

knowing that we have a powerful Friend. And their hope comes from knowing that the Helper has come.

In the days when we as a nation are tempted to think we are invincible, all-powerful, and able to stand on our own, it is good to remember that if the fledgling United States of America had not had a powerful friend in France, the odds are good that the cause would have been lost. Isn't it good to know that, as disciples of Jesus Christ, attempting to be his body in the world, we have a powerful Friend who comes to stand with us? Be of good cheer! The Helper is on the way!

"... the holy catholic church, the communion of saints"

> [To] all those who in every place call on the name of our Lord Jesus Christ, both their Lord and ours. (I Cor. 1:2)

An Outpost of Heaven

Let's face it: There are some things in the creed that are hard to believe, and sometimes this is one of them. Sometimes it's hard to believe in "the holy catholic church, the communion of saints."

Oh, it's easy enough when you spiritualize the church as the mystical union of all those who believe in Christ, but when you bring it down to earth and look at it in real places; when you get to know the history of its failures and compromises with evil; when you get involved in this huge, hulking institution with all its denominational differences, its budgets and committees, its confusion and debate; when you look around and see it filled with folks like us— doesn't it stretch your imagination to say *this* is the holy catholic church? *This* is the communion of saints? Aren't there times when it seems that the church is a lot like Noah's ark? The only way to stand the stench on the inside is to remember the storm on the outside.

I am well aware of the weaknesses of the church. I know the problems of our own denomination, of this local church, better than anyone else in this room. I've read some of the books and articles that describe our failures. I've seen the effects of our compromises of the gospel. I've wept over our failures. I stand before you as one who has faced the reality of the church as we experience it but who still can say, "I believe in the church." I still believe that it is holy and catholic and that it represents the communion of saints. Let me share what this means for me.

I believe the church is *holy*. There's a word we don't use very often. At its best, the word *holy* conjures up images of esoteric monks drifting silently through the halls of ancient monasteries. At its worst, it can carry the image of artificial spirituality and phony piety. Who really wants to be holy anyway?

> *"To say that the church is holy is to say that ordinary people like us have been called out by God for God's purpose."*

Biblically, the word *holy* simply describes something or someone who is set apart for the purpose of God. In the Old Testament, the Temple was holy. Why? Because it was set apart for the worship of God. The people of the covenant were holy. Why? Because they sensed a special calling to fulfill God's purpose. In the New Testament, the Greek word for "church" is *ecclesia,* which literally means "the called out ones." To say that the church is holy is to say that ordinary people like us have been called out by God for God's purpose, the way the president calls someone to be an ambassador to another country. The people of faith are called to bear witness to God's great act of love and grace in Jesus Christ. We are chosen, not for privilege, but for service, to be a living model of the kingdom of God, which is being fulfilled on earth even as it is already fulfilled in heaven.

Do you remember the television show "Hogan's Heroes"? It was a preposterous television comedy about a team of soldiers who were held in a German prisoner of war camp during World War II, and of how they were actually undermining the whole system from the inside out. That's not a bad picture for the church. C. S. Lewis called the world "enemy-occupied territory," and said that Christianity is the story of how "the rightful ruler" has landed in disguise and is calling all of us to a campaign of sabotage.

"Hogan's Heroes" is satire, but the historical situation was deadly serious. The institutional church failed its exams in Nazi Germany, copping out and going along with the anti-Semitism of the Third Reich. But don't forget the story of the confessing church, which stood out like a flickering candle of truth and justice in the darkness of oppression and death. One historian called it "an enclave of heaven in the middle of hell." That's exactly what the church is called to be: people who are distinctively different because in the middle of this world they live in ways that are consistent with the kingdom of God—an enclave of heaven in the middle of hell.

The Rosa Valdez Center is a place like that. It is a preschool and day-care center for the children of destitute families in the inner city of Tampa. Because the Center provides love, care, and learning for the children, their parents are able to find jobs, to establish homes, and to become productive parts of society. After hearing the director describe the magnitude of the need and the difficulty of the work, I asked what keeps her going. She replied, "This is the Lord's work, and somebody has to do it. As long as the job needs to be done,

I'll be here." That's holy. That's a sense of calling. That's what it means to be set apart for the purpose of God.

> *"We will never fully discover who God has called us to be until we discover it in relationship with people of other races, nations, cultures, and political or economic systems."*

Perhaps the most common question I hear about the Apostles' Creed is this: "Why do we say 'holy catholic church'? I thought we were Protestants." The answer is very simple. There are two ways to use the word *catholic*. If you talk about the Roman Catholic Church with a capital "C," you are talking about a particular, witnessing part of the body of Christ, based in Rome and presided over by the pope. But if you say "catholic" with a small "c," you are using the word as an adjective that means universal, describing all of us, everywhere, bearing witness to Jesus Christ. And, believe it or not, with all of the bickering among the distant cousins, the church of Jesus Christ is still one, universal family. The church, at its best, is catholic—transcending all boundaries of nationality, race, language, culture, and political and economic systems.

I never felt the catholicity of the church more powerfully than I did at the World Methodist Conference in Nairobi, Kenya, in 1986. I still remember the opening communion service: watching the banners of churches from ninety different nations process into the hall; hearing the words, "This is my body, broken for you" spoken at the same time in dozens of different languages; breaking the common loaf and sharing a common cup with men and women of every color, language and culture. I still remember the chills that went down my spine on Sunday morning at the Anglican Cathedral when we sang the "Te Deum" and came to the phrase, "The Church in all the world praises you." I still remember the way we shared the vision of justice and peace for the broken world in which we serve. I still feel the bond of faith and friendship that binds us to one another. I remember the banners of the churches from East Germany and West Germany, standing side by side throughout that conference. Who would ever have guessed that four years later the Berlin Wall would be open, the barbed wire torn down, and the people reunited?

We will never fully discover who God has called us to be until we discover it in relationship with people of other races, nations, cultures, and political or economic systems. The kingdom of heaven looks more like the United Nations than the D.A.R. I believe more deeply than ever before in the "catholic" church.

> *"Paul said that everyone who is committed to Christ is called to be a saint."*

I also believe that the church is the communion of saints. Now, do you want something that is almost impossible to believe? Just look around you this morning. Look at the preacher. Look at the choir. Look at the people behind and in front of you. Now, say to yourself, *"This* is the communion of saints."

Paul said that everyone who is committed to Christ is called to be a saint, which was saying a lot when you consider the problems of the church in Corinth. Peter Marshall called us "the saints of the rank and file"—

ordinary folks who by God's grace are called, chosen, and empowered to be God's people, the body of Christ in the world.

When was the last time you heard someone say, "The church is full of hypocrites"? I'm so weary of hearing this that I'm considering the response, "So, what else is new?" I know there are persons in the church who don't live up to their calling; I'm one of them. I know there are persons who can be mean and nasty and downright impossible. But I also know that my life has been richly blessed by the fellowship of the saints. I thought of some of them this week.

I remembered a Sunday school teacher who welcomed me to her first-grade Vacation Bible School class. I can still taste her Ritz crackers and cherry Kool-Aid. I can remember the way she stuck pictures of Jesus on a flannelgraph board. She let me know that the church was a place where I was loved.

I remember a car salesman who tried to teach a Sunday school class of seventh-grade boys, most of the time with minimal success! I don't remember much of what he taught us, but I do remember that we were very difficult to teach. By God's grace, I believe he forgave us. And by God's grace, he was there every week, and we knew he cared.

I remember a retired Methodist preacher who sat on the end of the second pew in my home church. When we came into the sanctuary, we'd find him already sitting there, his head bowed down on the pew in front of him in prayer. I can still hear his voice and feel his bony hand on mine when he prayed, before I went off to college, that I'd become a Methodist preacher.

I am who I am today because of the communion of saints, because of ordinary folks through whom I experienced the love of God. I believe in this affirmation, which hurls us out into the infinity of eternal life, because I have experienced it right here on earth. And I've experienced it here, with you. Every time I look out at this congregation I feel like the person who was lucky enough to be playing the tuba when it started raining silver dollars. Right here, right now, this is the communion of saints.

Let's face it: Sometimes we get discouraged or disappointed; sometimes it's tough to believe. But now and then we catch a glimpse of what the church is called to be, and when we do, we can still find faith to believe that the church is holy, catholic, and the communion of saints.

> *Happy are those whose transgression is forgiven, whose sin is covered. (Ps. 32:1)*

Extraordinary Forgiveness for Ordinary Sin

Happy are those whose transgression is forgiven,
   whose sin is covered. . . .
While I kept silence, my body wasted away
   through my groaning all day long. . . .
   My strength was dried up as by the heat of summer.
Then I acknowledged my sin to you,
   and I did not hide my iniquity;
I said, "I will confess my transgressions
      to the LORD,"
   and you forgave the guilt of my sin.
(Ps. 32:1, 3-5)

Those words are not true because they are in the Bible. They are in the Bible because they are true—true to the real stuff of our lives; true to the most profound understandings of human psychology and mental health; true to everything we know about forgiveness and sin.

A preacher friend of mine owned a small farm in the hills of Tennessee. One time when he went up to the farm he took a drink of water, and it tasted terrible. He knew something was wrong because the spring water was usually fresh and clean, right out of the Tennessee hills. He went down to the spring house, dug up all the weeds, cleared away the accumulated dust and trash, and even painted the outside of the spring house. It looked better, but the water still tasted terrible. Finally, he called a repairman, who was able to reach all the way down to the bottom of the well and found the decaying carcass of a huge bullfrog that had fallen into the well and died. The point of his story is that it doesn't matter how much you clean up the spring house until you get the bull frog out of the well.

> *"The Bible identifies the bullfrog in the well of human experience as sin. . . . And the answer that God offers is forgiveness."*

When the early Christians began formulating what became the Apostles' Creed, they knew that it would not be enough to merely paint the spring house, to deal with the surface issues of life. They knew that they would have to go all the way to the bottom of the human soul and deal with the bullfrog that pollutes the flow of life, freedom, and wholeness. And so they said, "I believe . . . in the forgiveness of sins."

The Bible identifies the bullfrog in the well of human experience as sin. The selfishness that pollutes human relationships, the tragic twist that causes us to follow our own way instead of the way of God, the separation that we feel from God, the alienation that divides the human family, the greed that corrupts societies, the violence that rips the fabric of life—the Bible calls it all sin. And the answer that God offers is forgiveness. To see what that forgiveness looks like, let's look at one of the most dramatic stories in the Bible: King David's affair with Bathsheba.

David was a shepherd from the hill country, but God made him the king of Israel. God gave him everything he could ask for, and more. Late one summer afternoon when he was walking on his balcony, he looked down into his neighbor's garden and saw Bathsheba taking a bath. The narrator records that David noticed she was beautiful. Most of us would have noticed that, too. She was the wife of Uriah, one of David's soldiers on the battlefield. David brought Bathsheba to the palace, had sex with her, and sent her home.

David might have gotten away with what he had done, but Bathsheba discovered that she was pregnant. In the best soap opera tradition, David called Uriah back from the battlefield to give him a report on the battle. He figured he could send Uriah home to Bathsheba and everyone would assume that the baby was Uriah's child. What David didn't count on was that Uriah was a man of great integrity.

When David tried to send Uriah home, Uriah said, "Oh, my King, all the soldiers are out in the field, away from their families and their homes. How can I betray their trust and go home to my wife?" (II Sam. 11:11, paraphrased). David said, "Oh, go on!" But Uriah refused and spent the night outside David's door. The next day David invited Uriah to dinner and got him drunk, but Uriah still refused to go home, and instead spent the night with the palace guards. The next morning he went back to the field, never having seen his wife.

David wasn't finished. He sent word to the general to attack and to put Uriah on the front line. The next day the word came back that Uriah had been killed in battle. David brought Bathsheba to the palace and married her. She gave birth to the child, and the king thought he had covered his tracks.

> "Our experience of God's forgiveness begins
> . . . in that silent space in our own souls
> where we sense the Spirit of God pointing
> a finger at us."

But Samuel records, "The thing that David had done displeased the LORD" (II Sam. 11:27), which must be one of the great understatements of scripture! The Lord sent Nathan, the prophet, to David. In one of the most dramatic scenes in the Old Testament, the prophet pointed his finger at the king and said, "Thou art the man!" (It's hard to beat the power of the Elizabethan English on that line!) The prophet predicted the tragic, human consequences of David's sin, consequences that even God's forgiveness could not entirely wipe out. The king fell on his knees before the prophet and confessed, "I have sinned against the Lord." Then Nathan spoke the words of absolution, "The Lord forgives you" (see 12:13).

Our sin may not be as sinister or as colorful as King David's, but our experience of God's forgiveness begins at the same place: in that silent space in our own souls where we sense the Spirit of God pointing a finger at us and hear God saying, "You are the one." Forgiveness begins when we sing with the spiritual, "It's me, it's me, O Lord, standing in the need of prayer." The word of scripture, confirmed by human psychology, is that "if we say that we have no sin, we deceive ourselves. . . . If we confess our sins, he who is faithful and just will forgive us our sins and cleanse us from all unrighteousness" (I John 1:8-9).

I saw a powerful illustration of this principle in a movie several years ago. The movie, *Ordinary People,* starred Mary Tyler Moore as a sophisticated, suburban woman who lived inside the plastic veneer of her successful life and refused to acknowledge the pain, hurt, and torment going on in her soul. Her husband and son face their pain, acknowledge their faults, and open their lives to each other. She struggles with whether to let go or hold on, to release herself or stay in bondage. As I watched this movie, a voice inside me wanted to shout back at the screen, "For God's sake, let go!" But she won't. She clicks her suitcase shut, closes the door, and never experiences the love and healing that her husband and son have to offer. The title of the movie is disturbingly accurate: *Ordinary People.* They were just ordinary people, like you and me, who refused to acknowledge their need, their pain, their sin, and thereby missed out on the forgiveness, healing, and wholeness that God offers.

John 21:15-19 tells the wonderful post-resurrection story of the risen Christ meeting the disciples for breakfast on the beach. After fishing all night without catching a thing, they wade onto shore and find Jesus, preparing breakfast over a charcoal fire. The fire is a key to the story. It was around a small fire like this one that Peter denied that he knew who Jesus was. There is no way Peter could have faced his Master beside that fire without facing the memory of his failure.

As the sun rises, Jesus turns to Peter and asks, "Peter, do you love me?" Peter responds, "Lord, you know I love you." Jesus says, "Feed my sheep," and a second time asks, "Peter, do you love me?" Again, Peter answers, "Yes, Lord, I love you." Jesus says again, "Feed my sheep." Then a third time, just like the three times Peter denied him in the courtyard, Jesus asks, "Peter, do you love me?" And Peter cries, "Lord, you know everything—you know the way I failed you. You know my night of defeat, you know my sin—you know all of that, and yet you know that I love you." And the third time, Jesus tells him to care for his sheep.

> *"Forgiveness doesn't mean that the past is canceled. . . . But forgiveness opens a new future."*

I hear three truths about sin and forgiveness in this story. First, Jesus did for Peter something Peter could never do for himself. The only way for Peter to find healing was for him to experience forgiveness from the one against whom he had sinned.

Second, Jesus forgave Peter by giving him back his future. When Jesus said, "Feed my sheep," it was like saying, "Peter, here's your old job back again. Here's your calling, given back to you fresh and clean and new. Go ahead; fulfill your calling: Feed my sheep." To be forgiven is to be given an open future. Forgiveness doesn't mean that the past is canceled. Peter could never wipe away the memory of his night in the courtyard anymore than David could wipe away all of the consequences of his sin with Bathsheba. But forgiveness opens a new future. It means that we no longer are imprisoned by our past. Forgiveness sets us free to fulfill the calling that God places on our lives.

My third discovery was that most of us are more familiar with the story of Peter's denial in the courtyard than we are with his forgiveness on the beach. We know the story of his sin better than we know the story of his forgiveness. Could it be that we identify with his failure but have not found his healing? It may be that some of us are ready to move from the darkness of the courtyard of denial into the sunrise of forgiveness.

I believe in the forgiveness of sin. That forgiveness begins when I confess my sin, acknowledge my fault, and recognize my need. That forgiveness is accomplished when we hear Jesus say, "Go, feed my sheep."

"the resurrection of the body and the life everlasting"

But in fact Christ has been raised from the dead, the first fruits of those who have died. (I Cor. 15:20)

A Place for You

I remember the day the call came; I can still hear the voice on the other end of the line. The twenty-one-year-old son of a fellow pastor, one of my "fathers" in the ministry, was dead, killed when his truck slammed into a telephone pole. My mind immediately flew back to the hours I had spent with him when he was a kid in the youth program in my first pastoral appointment. It was ruthlessly unfair, unbelievably painful.

I joined several hundred other preachers, family members, and friends for the worship service, where we remembered that young man and affirmed our faith in Christ. When the service was over I went to the parsonage, a home filled with the mementos of solid, healthy, joyful family life. My friend and I met at the door. He wrapped his arms around me, and we wept together. I said what we all say, "Is there anything I can do for you?" knowing that there is absolutely nothing any human being can do to soften that kind of pain, except to share it. But I shall never forget what he said: "Jim, the next time you preach on the resurrection, thump the Book one time for me."

As we consider together the conclusion of the Apostles' Creed, I want to "thump the Book" one more time for my friend and for his son and for a host of others with whom I have shared the brutal reality of death. "I believe in the resurrection of the body and the life everlasting." I don't understand it; I can't fully explain it; but I believe it more profoundly than I have ever believed it before.

In fact, *believe* isn't strong enough. It doesn't describe what we feel when we confront death and claim the promise of the resurrection. The early church might have felt that way, too. A hundred or so years after the Apostles' Creed was formulated, the Council of Nicea tried once again to spell out what the church believed. They changed the verb from *believe* to *expect,* so that the affirmation became, "I expect the resurrection of the body and the life of the world to come." When Beethoven set it to music in the "Mass in C," he had the chorus and orchestra repeat the statement, each time more boldly than before: "et expecto, et expecto, resurrectionem."

I remember standing beside my grandfather's hospital bed, waiting for the line on the monitor to go flat, waiting for his last labored breath, humming Beethoven's setting of that phrase in the back of my brain: "et expecto." I watched him die in expectation of the resurrection of that weakened body and the new life of the world to come.

> *"[The Bible] says that even this body—weak, frail, finite, subject to sin and death—will have a part in the new life of the world to come."*

The most daring phrase in this affirmation is "resurrection of the body." It shocked the Corinthian Christians.

They were Greeks who believed in the immortality of the soul, which meant that when one dies the soul, which is good, escapes the mortal body, which is evil, and soars off to a spiritual realm.

Some of that has seeped into Christianity, but the Bible as a whole doesn't buy it. The Hebrews believed that God created humans as whole beings. Body, mind, soul, spirit—whatever labels you use, they are all tangled up together. Our bodies are part of who we are; there is no such thing as a disembodied soul. In one sense, the Bible is ruthlessly materialistic. It says that even this body—weak, frail, finite, subject to sin and death—will have a part in the new life of the world to come.

That was a revolutionary idea to the people in Corinth. They couldn't help asking, "How are the dead raised? With what kind of body do they come?" (I Cor. 15:35). Paul responds with a simple lesson in horticulture: A seed is planted in the ground. It doesn't sprout unless it dies. When it grows, it has a totally different appearance than it had as a seed, but it is still wheat or corn or grain. That's how it is, Paul said, with the resurrection of the dead.

> So it is with the resurrection of the dead. What is sown is perishable, what is raised is imperishable. It is sown in dishonor, it is raised in glory. It is sown in weakness, it is raised in power. It is sown in a physical body, it is raised a spiritual body. . . . Just as we have borne the image of the man of dust, we will also bear the image of the man of heaven. (I Cor. 15:42-44, 49)

Paul used the analogy of seeds. I like caterpillars. I love the old story of the two grungy, earthy caterpillars who were crawling along in the dust. A butterfly soared off into the sunlight overhead. One caterpillar said to the other,

"You'll never get me up in one of those things!" But it will! One day that caterpillar will curl up on a branch and "die." But when springtime comes, and the sun begins to warm the earth, the Monarch will burst out in all its glory and flutter off into the sun, its new body soaring into the new world to come.

> *"Eternal life will be the completion of what we are now becoming, the fulfillment of everything we believe, dream, hope, desire, and love."*

Paul talked about seeds, and I like caterpillars. But Jesus used a word picture that is even more homey. At the last supper, with the shadow of death looming over him, he told the disciples: "In my Father's house there are many dwelling places. If it were not so, would I have told you that I go to prepare a place for you? . . .[After I go and prepare a place for you,] I will come again and will take you to myself, so that where I am, there you may be also" (John 14:2-3).

I have a special memory of the day we moved into our last parsonage. Everything was in chaos. Boxes were stacked everywhere. People were racing around all over the place, trying to get the truck unloaded before the afternoon thunderstorm hit. Suddenly, we realized that we had lost track of five-year-old Debbie. We started looking around, and I found her. The little table and chair that her grandfather had built for her mother when she was that age had been placed in Debbie's new room. There she was, sitting in her chair, at her table, in her room, reading one of her books. Everything else was in confusion, but she had found her place.

Psychologists tell us that every human being needs a sense of his or her own space. In their book *Self, Space and Shelter,* Norma Newmark and Patricia Thompson write: "Housing . . . is the place to be and the place to become what each person alone or as part of a group is uniquely capable of becoming."

Each of us can imagine our place, a particular room that is the extension of who and what we are. Mine is a wood paneled study with lots of bookshelves, a fireplace at one end, a large bay window looking out on the lake, and a big overstuffed chair. I can even smell it: all brown and leathery, my own little corner of the world. My wife's psychological room would be light and green, filled with plants and sunshine. She'd be miserable in my room; that's why each of us has our own.

If we had time to go around the congregation today, we'd find that each person could describe his or her imaginary room—a room that is the extension of your personality, the fulfillment of your identity. For just a moment, picture it in your mind. See it, feel it, smell it—your place to be and to become. Just as we cannot think of ourselves without a body, so we also have a hard time imagining ourselves without a sense of place.

Jesus promises the spiritual expression of that psychological reality. Whatever we experience after death, Jesus promises that we will have a room of our own—not in a physical, literal sense, but in the sense that eternal life will be the completion of what we are now becoming, the fulfillment of everything we believe, dream, hope, desire, and love.

> *"Jesus, the master architect . . . has gone ahead to prepare a place for me."*

I recently visited with a family who had just moved back into a house that they had remodeled. Before the remodeling, the house had been adequate, comfortable, but there were ways in which it just wasn't "them." They hired an architect, who spent a considerable amount of time getting to know them, talking about how they lived and what they did. He drew the plans, and they went to work, rebuilding the place from the ground up. When I stepped into the new home, I immediately said, "This is really you!"

That's how heaven will be. Jesus, the master architect, the one who knows me better than I know myself, has gone ahead to prepare a place for me. He will come again to take me with him into that place, which will be the perfect fulfillment of all that I am now becoming. I don't expect a lot of surprises after death. I expect everyone to look at each other in our new bodies and say, "Ah! That's really you! More fully and completely you than you have ever been before." It's the "you" that you can live with forever.

Seeds, caterpillars, rooms—they are all finite pictures of the infinite mystery of the Christian faith. No wonder Paul said:

Listen, I will tell you a mystery! We will not all die, but we will all be changed, in a moment, in the twinkling of an eye, at the last trumpet. For the trumpet will sound, and the dead will be raised imperishable, and we will be changed. For this perishable body must put on imperishability, and this mortal body must put on immortality. When this perishable body puts on imperishability, and this mortal body puts on immortality, then the saying that is written will be fulfilled:
"Death has been swallowed up in victory."
"Where, O death, is your victory?
Where, O death, is your sting?"

The sting of death is sin, and the power of sin is the law. But thanks be to God, who gives us the victory through our Lord Jesus Christ. (I Cor. 15:51-57)

I believe—no, I expect—the resurrection of the body and the life everlasting. When we've said that, there is nothing else to say.

Suggested Reading

Barclay, William. *The Apostles' Creed for Everyman*. New York: Harper & Row, 1962.

Barth, Karl. *Credo*. New York: Scribner's, 1962.

Beethoven, Ludwig. "Mass in C," Op. 86, Angel Records, S-36775.

Capon, Robert Farrar. *Hunting the Divine Fox*. New York: Seabury, 1973.

Hauerwas, Stanley, and William Willimon. *Resident Aliens: Life in the Christian Colony*. Nashville: Abingdon Press, 1989.

Jones, E. Stanley. *Abundant Living*. Nashville: Abingdon Press, 1970.

Küng, Hans. *On Being a Christian*. Garden City, New York: Doubleday, 1966.

Lewis, C. S. *Mere Christianity*. New York: Macmillan, 1964.

Littell, Franklin, ed. *The German Church Struggle and the Holocaust*. Detroit: Wayne State University Press, 1978.

Marshall, Catherine. *The Helper*. Waco, Tex.: Chosen Books, 1978.

Phillips, J. B. *Your God Is Too Small*. New York: Macmillan, 1967.

Read, David H. C. *The Faith Is Still There*. Nashville: Abingdon Press, 1981.

Read, David H. C. "Sermons." Madison Avenue Presbyterian Church, 921 Madison Ave., New York, NY 10021.

————. "Tohu-Bohu and the Spirit of God," 36 (May 30, 1982). Madison Avenue Presbyterian Church, 921 Madison Ave., New York, NY 10021.

————. "A Big Enough God," 37 (June 6, 1982). Madison Avenue Presbyterian Church, 921 Madison Ave., New York, NY 10021.

Sayers, Dorothy. *Creed or Chaos?* New York: Harcourt, Brace & Co., 1949.

Seamands, David A. "Born, Suffered, Died—Everyman's Story" (November 2, 1969). Wilmore United Methodist Church, Wilmore, KY.

Sparks, Allister. *The Mind of South Africa.* New York: Alfred A. Knopf, 1990.

Sweet, Leonard I. "Not All Cats Are Gray: Beyond Liberalism's Uncertain Faith." *The Christian Century* (June 23-30, 1982): 721ff.

Trotter, Mark. "In Him Was Life" (April 3, 1983). First United Methodist Church, 2111 Camino del Rio South, San Diego, CA 92108.

————. "A Room of Your Own" (May 29, 1983). First United Methodist Church, 2111 Camino del Rio South, San Diego, CA 92108.

————. "Sermons." First United Methodist Church, 2111 Camino del Rio South, San Diego, CA 92108.